DWAYNE the Farmer has a Garden

Dwayne A. Jones

Copyright© 2024 Dwayne A. Jones

All rights reserved.

No part of this book may be reproduced, stored in a retrieval system, or transmitted in any form or by any means, electronic, mechanical, photocopying, recording, scanning, or otherwise, without the prior written permission of the publisher.

Illustrated by Creative Next
Layout Design by Nonon Tech & Design

ISBN: 979-8-9905735-7-4 (Paperback)
ISBN: 979-8-9905735-6-7 (Hardback)

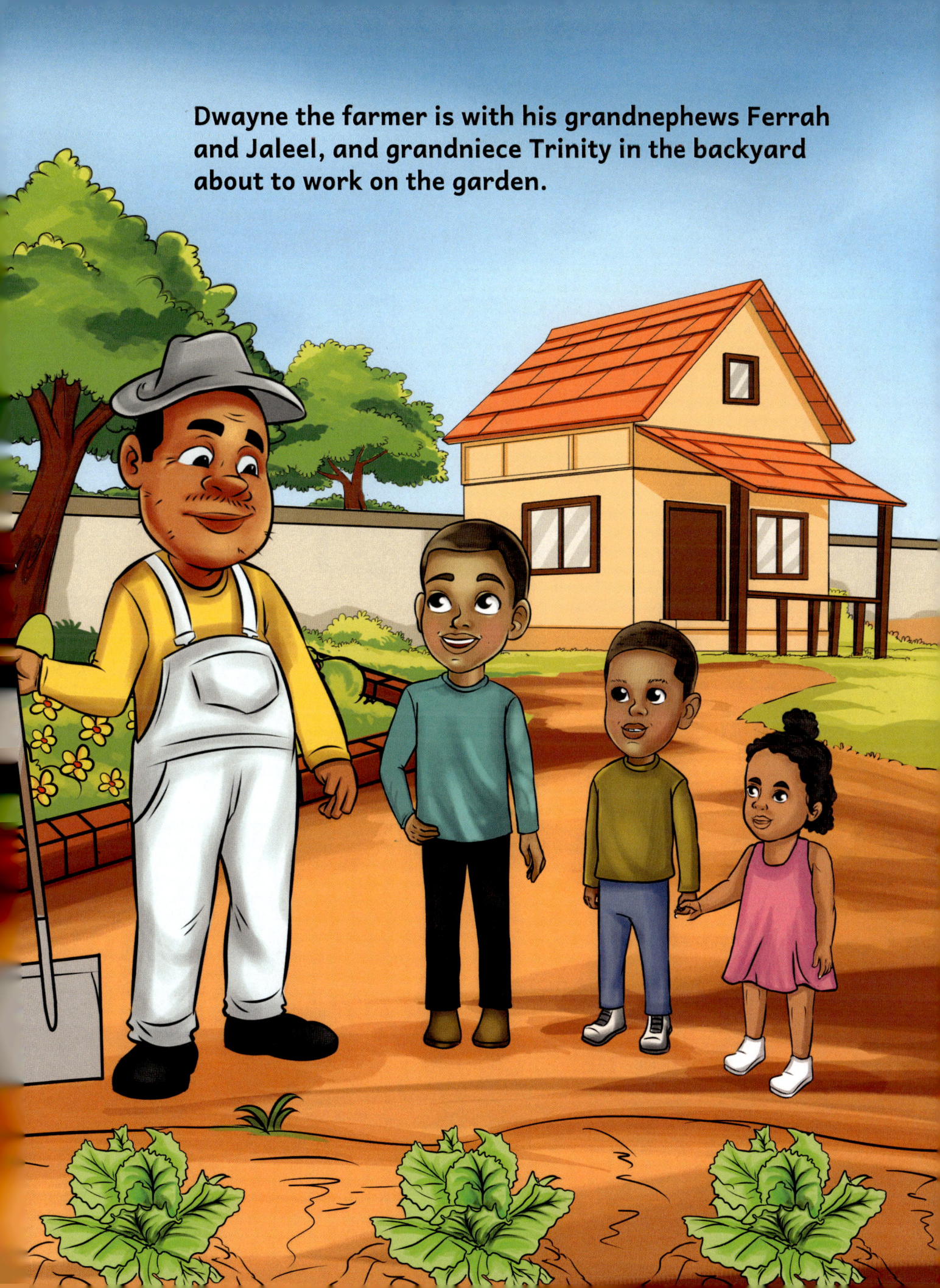

Dwayne the farmer is with his grandnephews Ferrah and Jaleel, and grandniece Trinity in the backyard about to work on the garden.

Dwayne first asks Ferrah to show his muscles and Ferrah lifts both arms and flexes his muscles. Dwayne the farmer says, "Oh my, you have big muscles for a little guy." Jaleel says, "Me too!" and Trinity says, "Me too!", as Dwayne laughs.

They all walk over to the first plants – tomatoes.
Dwayne asks, "Who likes tomatoes?"
Trinity replies, "Me! Oh me!"

Dwayne the farmer tells Trinity to pick a red tomato and a green tomato, and she says, "OK".

Trinity then asks, "What does the difference in color mean?" At the same time, she hands Dwayne the two tomatoes. He explains, "The red tomato is fully grown and ripe, but the green tomato is not fully ripe. You can still fry it and eat it or put it in the window and it will turn red."

Jaleel grabs an ear of corn and asks, "What's this?" Ferrah tells them, "I know what that is, Uncle Dwayne. That's corn!" Dwayne says, "You are absolutely right." Jaleel adds, "I like corn" and Trinity nods, "Me too."

Next, they all walk over the greens growing in the garden. Ferrah says, "This looks like grass" and they all laugh. Dwayne says, "Yes, greens kind of look like grass but when you cook them, they are delicious. I'll pick some greens and have your mothers cook some with cornbread."

Dwayne the farmer reaches down and digs up some carrots and says, "Carrots usually grow underground, and you don't see them until you pull them up."
Ferrah says, "Ohhhh! I see the long orange carrot now."
Trinity nods, "Me too."

Dwayne says, "Let's go over here and pick out some watermelons from the watermelon patch."
Jaleel is excited, "I like watermelon!"
Trinity agrees, saying "Me too!"

Ferrah walks over to the watermelon patch and picks one off the vine and starts to carry it to the wagon. Dwayne asks, "Ferrah, are you sure you can carry it by yourself?" Ferrah nods, "I got it, Uncle Dwayne, I got it."

After putting the watermelon in the wagon, Ferrah adds, "I have muscles, remember?" Dwayne laughs and says, "I almost forgot. Yes, you do have big muscles for a little guy."

Dwayne says, "Let's get some strawberries and call it a day." He points to the strawberry patch.

Jaleel says, "Oh, I really like strawberries!" and they all run to the patch.

Dwayne picks a strawberry and eats one and the children ask if they eat some strawberries too. Dwayne says, "Sure, but make sure you put some in the wagon for your basket to take home."

Ferrah, Jaleel, and Trinity start eating some strawberries and putting others in the wagon.

Dwayne tells Ferrah to pull the wagon back to the house so they can wash the fruit and vegetables. Ferrah starts pulling the wagon; Trinity and Jaleel decide to help by pushing from the back.

When they get back to the house, Dwayne washes the vegetables and fruits in the sink as Ferrah, Jaleel, and Trinity watch.

Dwayne asks Trinity to bring three baskets over to the counter and she trots over to the corner and gets three baskets. Jaleel asks, "What are the baskets for?" Ferrah says, "He told us we can take what we picked home." Dwayne nods, "You are absolutely correct!" Ferrah, Jaleel, and Trinity all scream, "Yeahhhhh!"

Dwayne stacks the vegetables and fruits in each basket and tells them, "We are almost finished."
Jaleel asks, "What's next?"

Made in the USA
Middletown, DE
09 January 2026